LOST
PSYCHOLOGY'S EMPTY
PROMISES
Why Your SOUL Is Rarely Treated In A Therapy Session
Dr. Paul J. Young

LOST

Psychology's Empty Promises

- *How Psychology Missed The Soul*

- *How Most Everyone In Therapy Is Being Cheated*

Dr. Paul J. Young

Read This First

NO ONE DISCARDS A BOX OF DELICIOUS FRIED CHICKEN because it has bones. No way! You grab a piece, eat the meat and discard the bones.

So too with this book. Eat the meat - there is a lot here to chew on, think about, process and pray about. If you find any bones, discard them. Why waste all the meat because there are a few bones!

No book authored by a human is perfect, you know. We seek to write about infinite truth with only a finite understanding using a finite, limited language. I speak what I know has been revealed as accurately as possible without swerving to the left or right of the truth.

And that's it, isn't it - TRUTH.

I trust you find much in this book that will arrest your attention, and that you will line yourself with what is true, for the betterment of your soul.

There is no better way.

Table of Contents

1

Devastated!

S HE SAT THERE, HUNCHED OVER, broken and defeated. And her story shook me to the core.

Teresa was a well dressed, upper class woman who had lots of money, but no happiness. She had hit the bottom and came to see me as a last resort.

You see, I was Teresa's pastor (this was before I became Catholic) pastoring the largest church in the city - a church that pulled from all spectrums of society.

So Teresa sat there, telling her story.

She had been to 2-3 therapists, one a Christian. And none could help. They offered the typical Cognitive - Behavioral Therapy, which seemed to help at first, then the wheels came off.

Teresa could not keep a lid on her deep depression - a total devastation of what had happened to her daughter a few years before.

You see, her daughter, married to a successful pharmaceutical salesman, had it all, a beautiful , spacious home in the country and a growing, healthy nine month old baby girl who was the love of her life.

How could it get any better?

One day Teresa's daughter pulled into the garage after going shopping, grabbed her daughter and walked into her home surprising a burglar who was stealing things to pay for his drug habit. The young man pulled a gun, shot Teresa's daughter, pulled the wires to the phone and scurried out the door.

Badly bleeding, the daughter put her bloodied daughter on the floor, stepped out the front door and tried to get to a neighbor who lived a few hundred yards from her home.

She didn't make it.

Teresa's daughter fell into a ditch and died leaving her nine month daughter on the floor uncared for.

It wasn't until a neighbor drove by and saw the dead neighbor in the ditch that the police were called, and finally the mother was notified of this terrible incident.

Teresa was devastated. How? Why?

The grief was overwhelming, and she could never seem to quiet the pain of this incomparable loss.

So she decided to go for counseling.

The therapists she went to were well trained in their craft. And they new how to stop the thoughts and actions that so often torpedo a persons emotions and keep them in a prison of depression.

Though the sessions helped Teresa, they stopped short from bringing her the emotional and spiritual healing she needed.

Why?

Teresa had gone to some of the best trained therapists in the area. Money was no problem for her, so she sought out those who were highly recommended.

After all of this she decided to see me, broken, defeated and beside herself.

In her hopelessness she cried to me: "Pastor, what do I do now?"

I sat there for a moment grieving with this dear woman who had lost so much. Then I spoke:

"Teresa, I want you to promise to come and see me for 8 sessions. In these sessions I will give you a foundation upon which you can rebuild your hope and courage to live, and not only live, but live with a new sense of joy and peace."

She looked back at me, gave me a slight smile and replied: "I don't know if I can last that long, pastor."

She made a pact with me to give me a chance to right the ship and keep it from sinking. And as she left, I wondered if she would let me help her.

2

The Problem With Psychology Today

I KNEW ONE OF THE THERAPISTS Teresa went to - a Christian Psychologist who got her doctoral degree from Penn State and was a master of her trade. She often had a waiting list of people who wanted to see her.

This therapist demonstrated great listening skills (better than mine - I am more of a teacher than a counselor). And though Teresa was greatly helped by her, she, I believe, was not taken deep enough to find true and lasting healing.

Thus Teresa regressed into her depression and an unquieting sadness.

Why? Her Christian therapist had all the skills needed to help Teresa. Why the failure?

The difficulty I have often seen is that Christian therapists are not trained in TRUE CHRISTIAN THERAPY. Instead they learn a far more secularized approach to treating people with all kind of emotional issues.

Many Christians are attracted to CBT (Cognitive Behavioral Therapy) because, as Christians, they believe in thinking and acting right. It is part of their Christian foundational thinking.

Thoughts (interpretations of events) + **Actions** = **Emotions**

Change your thoughts and actions and you can change the way you feel.

You can even take CBT and use Scripture to guide right thinking and acting. So it seems that Cognitive Therapy blends greatly with Christian thought and practice. And, in many ways, it does.

Teresa was taken through this very effective approach of CBT.

I teach CBT in my books on depression, but this formula is only in volume 1 of my series of 3 books. Cognitive therapy, I believe, only takes people so far.

There are other doors to go through, other steps to bring healing to people who have had such a traumatic blow like Teresa.

Cognitive therapy, at least the way it is commonly taught and practiced, is not enough.

It was not enough for Teresa and it won't be enough for any person who has a soul.

That's ALL OF HUMANITY!

If it is true that CBT is not enough, why was my therapist friend taught that CBT was the best way to treat depression, anxiety and a host of other emotional issues?

The answer will surprise you.

3

True Psychology

WE ALL THINK WE KNOW WHAT PSYCHOLOGY IS. REALLY? Most do not know that the word comes from the Greek word "psyche," a word for the SOUL or

SOULcology.

Yet when you go to a psychologist or therapist, you will find that…

MANY HAVE NEVER STUDIED THE SOUL.

Because of this, most psychotherapists only take people part of the way to TOTAL recovery thus leaving their client only partially healed. They do not understand the true makeup of a person, that internal part that is left empty and alienated.

It is a shame that most universities where psychologists are trained never address this internal part of humanity.

Why?

It's simple.

They refuse to study the soul, that very thing that psychology (SOUL-cology - the study of the soul) should be studying. But, and get this… it is OFF LIMITS at most universities.

They avoid this study due to an antagonism against religion and…

Any Mention That Brings
GOD
Into the Picture.

What happens?

In avoiding the study of the soul, they take those suffering from depression or any other emotional difficulty only part of the way to healing and don't bring TOTAL Relief.

I wrote a series of books on depression (Dr. Paul's TOTAL Relief - Depression). These include workbooks and helpful "YES!" Cards to counter what too many therapists offer their clients. Many of these therapists are Christians who are swept up in a more secular approach rather than leading each client on a pathway that will open their souls to God and his unmatched presence and love.

You can see these books at <u>DrPaulYoung.com</u>.

I know that in my doctoral studies, the emphasis was too often on a more secular approach that did not exclude God, but it didn't really study the soul and how to bring healing on this deeper level. It was assumed that, as Christians, we would be Christian in our practice. But there was no serious study of the soul itself. To me, that was sad.

The Psalmist said:

> *Like a deer that yearns for the running streams, so my SOUL is yearning for you, my God.*
>
> Psalm 42

19

Teresa had learned how to think and act - reinterpreting each event so that she didn't feel bad and taking actions steps that reinforced those new thoughts.

But that was it. Religion was kept out of it even by a Christian therapist. She didn't want to mix religion with proven ways to bring healing, following the path of CBT.

Thus she short-changed Teresa - not on purpose, mind you. The study of the soul was not part of her therapeutic study at Penn State.[1]

I wanted to introduce Teresa to TRUE PSYCHOLOGY so that her SOUL would be changed, renewed and brought back to life.

---

[1] I am not advocating that Penn State in not professional in their approach to preparing psychologists. It is an outstanding university.

4

Empty Promises

TERESA HAD BEEN GIVEN AN EMPTY PROMISE. "Think and act right and you will feel right." What she was taught was true - to a point. In my first volume, Dr. Paul's TOTAL RELIEF - Depression, I focus on CBT therapy. And I made sure that Teresa understood it fully.

But she needed more.

She needed to be treated with true SOULcology - the study and healing of the soul.

Almost without exception all of the secular universities teach a secular approach to psychology. And that makes sense, doesn't it? After all they are secular.

Yet, it would seem that any good university would seek to pursue truth. Somehow though, the study of God is bypassed and is off limits.

When I did my university studies, I did take a course in the Psychology of Religion and another in the Philosophy of Religion.

We studied Carl Jung (who believed that Jesus died for God's sin against Job) and Bertrand Russell who wrote, *Why I Am Not A Christian.* None of the course work would have helped me to believe in God or that God had any relevance to my life.

I also read Albert Camus, Jean - Paul Sartre and a host of other atheistic writers who, as Camus inferred: "To believe in God was to commit intellectual suicide."

So, on my campus there was no room for the Christian God including Jesus Christ. It was as if only ignorant people still believed in him. And that was back in the 60's!

Now, today, atheistic materialism has taken root, and those who believe in God and truly, deliberately practice that faith, are often shunted to the side and not given professorships or any place of influence.

So much for the truth.[2]

Thus the university campus studies humanity, but not a humanity that was created by God. They trumpet a psychology that, in the final analysis, is empty, void of the very essence that makes up psychology - the SOUL.
Sad?

You bet!

I admire many therapists who have learned their craft and do it exceedingly well, whether they are a person of faith or not.

You don't have to be a Christian to feed a hungry person on the streets. All humankind can do this with great honor. Nor does one need to be a Christian to give aid when a person is anxious, fearful or covered over with hopelessness or depression.

Yet, to feed the soul, one has to believe in that soul, that it is real and unique - something far different than the body alone - the material part of us. A person needs to also believe in what is immaterial.

---

2 If you want to have fun with me searching the truth, read my book, *If There Is A God, Whose God Is God?* Or *Who Designed The Designer* by Michael Augros - an in depth look at God.

Not anyone can feed the soul and give it the kind of food that restores it and make it strong, vibrant, whole and joyful again.

And this is where PSYCHOLOGY IS LOST TODAY, peddling empty promises that only go so far and are stopped short of bringing TOTAL healing - healing to the soul.

It happened to Teresa. And it may be happening to you or to others you know.

You may even be a psychologist or therapist who has studied hard and has a deep love for people but are shortchanging them without your knowledge.
So you ask:

What then is this SOUL that psychology has forgotten and shunted off to the side? If it is immaterial, how do we treat it?

5

What Is The Soul?

———————

YEARS AGO I BOUGHT A BOOK written by a cardiac doctor who practiced at Emery University Hospital in Atlanta. He called himself an agnostic regarding God, not knowing if there really was one or not.

This doctor kept copious notes of what patients told him after their heart operations. Of course, they were under anesthesia and where out cold. But, to his amazement some of his patients talked about viewing the operation from above the room.[3]

———————

[3] There are many other stories and accounts much like this one where people have "out of body" experiences during an operation, at death, etc. These accounts are not just rumors but verified accounts of what really occurred.

They told this doctor specific information that they could have not known unless they were in the room, above the doctor, peering down on the operation.

When one person talks to you about this, you can bypass it. But when many bring up that they saw the whole operation, he couldn't discount it.

There was something more to the body than just the material, physical part. This doctor concluded that humans had an immaterial part of them, what religion refers to as the soul.

We see this so ably presented by the Hebrew and Christian Scriptures.

You see, Adam and Eve were created in the image and likeness of God. No other creature was ever created in this way. Angels were not - though they are awesome spirits. Animals were not.   They have a soul that is material. Humans, however, have souls that are spiritual and eternal.

Because both animals and humans have souls, they can communicate with each other and understand each other on this soulish level.

But, animals were not created in the *image and likeness* of God. You do not see animals gather for church each week to worship the creator. Though, in their own way, they glorify God, they do not have the depth of relationship we, as humans, can have with our creator. Why? We are made of the same stuff, a god substance that is unique to all of creation.

The problem with men and women is that they too often live on the animal plane rather than on the God-relationship plane. They eat, have sex, play, build and do all sorts of things that are good. It's just that they do not really act human. For to be human, to be a TRUE MAN or WOMAN, is to have a relationship with the creator, to walk with him, as did Adam and Eve in the cool of the day.

Those who don't do that are not living up to their full human potential. Their souls are empty.

Everything today fights against this truly human potential.

For the last 500 years or so, humankind has been running in the opposite direction from God, torching their Christian base, seeking freedom from God just like Adam and Eve did.

Most studies in our universities and places of learning have led people down the dark pathway that ultimately dehumanized us and made us far less than what we really are.

Cosmology, anthropology, philosophy, psychology, and all the other "ologies", even many times theology, make humans a lost creature in space, searching for meaning.

The earth is not really special in the mass of the universe, we are told. Further, we only, by chance, happened to come from the slime of some molecules, forming life.

And here we are!

And if we are just a higher animal, this impacts our morals whereby everything is accepted…all the gold, glory, girls and guys.[4]

We see this today where the Ten Commandments and the moral code of the Bible has been thrown out, where those who are made from god-stuff can act and be free like those made with just animal-stuff, material only, no spirit that was meant to fly.

---

[4] You can read my two books on this subject, *Gold, Glory & Girls* for men or *Gold, Glory & Guys* for women. You can find them on my website, DrPaulYoung.com or on amazon.com.

This is why we feel a sense of separation, disenfranchised, alienated, alone in the universe, in our neighborhoods, in our homes, in ourselves as men and women.

No wonder the Google executive some years ago tried to get lost in wild sex and drugs. What else could dull the ache in his heart, deliver him from stress and boredom in his soul and give him a thrill that would help him escape his world. So he decided to move on the animal plane, getting all the sex and thrills his money could buy.

And he died doing it.

Yet, we are NOT animal, though there are many similarities. We are "gods" longing to have a relationship with THE GOD of the universe - god having fellowship with God, our souls filled with his presence.

Now, if you have never heard such talk before, let me assure you that I speak from the authority of the Church. Christianity has taught this clearly, and we need to humbly accept WHO WE ARE. It was one of the first disciples of Jesus who said:

> *We share in HIS DIVINE NATURE*
> II Peter 1:4

Saint Athanasius, the great bishop and theologian of the early Church, put it this way:

God became man that man might become god.

Let me tell you a parable so that you might more clearly understand.

Years ago, high in the Rockies, an eagle's egg somehow got loose from its nest, rolled down a ravine and came to rest in a turkey's nest. And there it lay, with the mother turkey sitting on it like the other turkey eggs.

Then one day it happened. All the eggs cracked open, and there were all the new turkeys. Yet one looked very different.

The turkey mother called him Tommy and spent more time with him helping him to eat the seeds and dig for worms (which he did not like very much). As Tommy grew older, he would look at times up into the sky at the eagles soaring freely in the heavens above.

"Wow! I wish I could do that," he said.

But his mother would chide him and tell him that he was just a turkey. "Get back and find those bugs and seeds," she would command him.

One day Tommy was by a stream drinking the water, and he saw a trout swimming by. Instinctively he moved to capture the trout with his powerful claws, snatching it from the water.

"Stop it!" His mother cried. Turkeys don't eat trout. What's gotten into you?"

Yet, Tommy still found himself looking into the sky, longing to fly, to be an eagle. And there were days that he would let out a loud screech, not the usual gobble that should come from a turkey.

Then one day an eagle spotted Tommy running around with the turkeys. He swooped down and got him to the side, saying: "What are you doing down here with these turkeys? You're an eagle."

"I am?" responded Tommy.

He knew he was different from all the others. And, he had dreamed of flying freely in the sky, eating trout, and being the king of the air.

So the eagle got Tommy to go up with him to a cliff overlooking the valley. He told Tommy that if he jumped off the cliff, he could fly, sail like all the other eagles.

Tommy, however, was afraid. All his life he had been told that he was a turkey. And he believed it. It was that belief that resulted in his turkey actions, eating seeds, worms, bugs… and gobbling.

So the great eagle gave Tommy a shove. Over the cliff he went, falling toward the valley below.

"Open your wings," screamed the eagle. "Flap them. You can do it. Soar!"

Tommy obediently opened his wings, still believing that he was a turkey. He began to flap them fearfully, trying to stop his rapid decent toward a certain death.
Then it happened.

Just before smashing into the jagged rocks below, his wings gave him a much needed lift, up, higher and higher into the open sky. In all the excitement he let out a screech, with a smile on his face that broadcasted his joy.

"I'm an eagle, I'm an eagle, I'm really an eagle," he declared!

And he sailed off with the other eagle to meet the other eagle friends who sailed in the open skies, eagles who knew who they were and were now glad that Tommy knew who he was.

There is this deep call within all of us, as men and women, to BE WHO WE ARE, to quit being a bunch of turkeys and to be eagles, to be SONS AND DAUGHTERS OF THE LIVING GOD - children of God, made of the same stuff he is made of, this "god fabric."

It is this call that haunts the average man and woman. They want freedom, but they seek to accomplish it on the animal level rather than break loose, jump off the cliff and learn to fly.

Those who wait upon the LORD will renew their strength; they will mount up with wings like eagles; they will run and not grow weary, they will walk and not faint.

Isaiah 40:31

If you could see yourself as God sees you, even as God made you, you would shudder in amazement. The Psalmist said in Psalm 139 and Psalm 8:

We are fearfully, awesomely and wonderfully made,
made a little lower than GOD.

We tend to compare ourselves to animals, but the gap between us and them is almost beyond measure. Instead, we are very close to God our maker, made up of the same stuff he is made of.

Yet it was from this high pinnacle that humankind fell. And that is why our souls are empty, and why they need to be inhabited by God.

We keep running after gold, glory, girls and guys rather than God.

This is why there is so much depression, anxiety, anger, stress, and loneliness…especially loneliness, the cry for a father, for Father God to be there, to be with us, and to walk day by day, moment by moment with us.

So what can be done about it? The soul must be brought into UNION with GOD.

But let's not get ahead of ourselves. First I need to demonstrate that all humans have a souls, persons that are both material and immaterial.

6

Evidence That We Have A Soul

———

It is certain as anything can be, Cebes, that the soul is immortal and imperishable, and the our souls will really exist in the next world.

Socrates, Plato's *Phaedo*

CAN I REALLY PROVE THAT THE SOUL EXISTS?[5]

I know that you may be snickering right now, thinking that I will use the Bible or some other religious writings to "prove" my points.

I could do that, but won't, at least initially. I believe that it is possible to demonstrate that the soul exists, and if it does,

———

[5] For an extensive study of the immaterial part of humanity read: *The IMMORTAL In You - How Human Nature Is More Than Science Can Say* by philosopher Michael Augros

SOULcologists (psychologists) should be treating the soul as it really is.

Let me show you the evidence.

I recall when I was a college minister on a University campus in California talking with students, I struck up a conversation with a young man about God, and he immediately challenged me that if I could prove there was a God he would believe.

I smiled and replied:

> *If you can prove YOU exist I will prove that God exists.*

He sat there for a moment in disbelief that I would ever challenge him in this way.

In one sense, what can you know for certain?

Scientists who study the universe know that it is made up of time, space and matter. Do they really know much if anything about them?

What is space? How far does it go? Where does it stop? If the universe does stop, what's on the other side? And time - are we passing through it or is it passing through us? How about matter? What exactly keeps that atom together (they say the "god" particle)?

We know so little and keep changing our thoughts on what we know.

So when I asked this student to prove he existed, he replied in a very predictable way.

> *Look.   You can see me, touch me.   I am here.   It's obvious.   Therefore I have proved I am in existence.*

> *But how do I know that we're not dreaming, that reality is not what you think it is,* I replied?

He sat there for a moment not sure what to say.   Then I smiled and told him I was having fun with him - playing thought games. And we both laughed.

I then went on to show him that he could prove he existed much like I would prove that God existed.

At this he was all ears.

Now the purpose of this book is not to prove the existence of God.[6] You can read my unusual approach in my book called, *If There Is A God, Whose God Is God?*

The purpose of this chapter is to demonstrate beyond reasonable doubt that there is a SOUL, that it exists and needs to be understood by psychologists so it can be treated with understanding and care.

For most of recorded history people have been **dualists** - agreeing that humans are both material and immaterial.

Then came the scientists who said:

If I can't see it I won't believe it.

SEE.

BELIEVE.

Sounds simple, doesn't it?

The difficulty is that science deals with the natural realm, and we are seeking to talk about the immaterial realm.

---

[6] Read this great book for further clarification: *Who Designed the Designer?: A Rediscovered Path to God's Existence* by Michael Augros

They can't see it. The reason is obvious. It is beyond the scope of their profession.

In this case, it is better to look at philosophy and what it teaches than the natural, physical realm of the scientist to see if dualism (the existence of a material and immaterial realm) is true.

You see, much of the world stands outside of our ability to see. Can you see time? No. Then why believe in it? Can you see an electron? No. Then why believe they exist?

Well, the answer to the electron is much like that of the soul. You can't see your soul, but you KNOW it is there. Why?

Let me give you a few thoughts.[7]

1. **You have a MIND that goes beyond your brain.** The physical, material brain is the way you process information, but to think of transcendent[8] things takes you beyond the elements of this physical brain.

---

[7] See J. P. Moreland, *The Soul - How We Know It's Real And Why It Matters* for a more complete examination of the evidence for the soul.

[8] Transcendent means surpassing others; preeminent or supreme, lying beyond the ordinary range of perception

The **BRAIN** has PHYSICAL PROPERTIES.

The **MIND** has MENTAL PROPERTIES and is trans-physical pointing to a SOUL and to a dualism that is both material and immaterial.

Thus, YOU are more than your brain since you can have self-conscious, conceptual, abstract and transcendent thoughts.

We can take out a ruler and measure the width and length of your brain. We can weigh it and calculate its mass. Yet as humans, we possess mental entities such as thoughts, desires, wills and sensations that are not measurable.

How do you measure a thought or any propositional content? You can't. That is why we are more than physical beings - a temporary association of molecules that will disband after death and be redistributed to make up other things. This is not only a troubling thought but not in line with the truth. If you are only a blob of molecules, then you are, in one sense, no different than a rock! To affirm this is to underscore our ultimate worthlessness, and that our lives are really meaningless.

But if you have a MIND, it means that you are more than matter. It demonstrates that you have a SOUL made up of material *and* immaterial (dualism), that you are more than a rock and thus have worth, meaning and purpose now and forever.

Just stop and think with me for a moment. You have the ability to reason with your intellect, to grasp UNIVERSALS which are **abstract things** like yellowness, redness, various shades of green, or a square always being equal sides with right angles. You also have the ability to grasp PARTICULARS which are **concrete things** like a tree, a blade of grass, a flower or a dog or any other singular object.

For example a red ball shows us what is universal (red) and particular (the ball - a particular, individual substance or thing). Although the ball, being a circle, may make me think of a universal because a circle is a universal thought. Circles can be any size from the smallest to the size of the universe!

You can see how my mind is working now, can't you? It's amazing, isn't it, that we can think beyond ourselves as we scrape the edges of the universe!

Spiders, birds, other insects and animals do some pretty amazing things. But they never look at a sunset and say: "Wow!" Their brains mechanically work in marvelous ways, but they do not ask questions like: "Why, How, When, Where, or What?" They are not capable of thinking of universals at all.

Though some animals and humans have a close DNA, the spread between them and us is almost infinite. For example, a chimp, whose DNA is close to ours, never gathers to worship the infinite or pause in thanksgiving for all its blessings especially those underserved. It's impossible for them, because they do not have a MIND that functions like the human mind, a soul that was created to imagine and dream great things, or make moral choices based on truth.

Such great universals as honesty, beauty, love and generosity connected to many virtues such as humility, chastity, temperance and kindness are just a small list of why humans have a MIND that functions in ways beyond the brain.

The body without a soul is just a corpse. Yet, because the soul can see[9] think and exist beyond the body, like the mind from the brain, it is then something of great value and worth treating by a therapist if their client is depressed, anxious or otherwise emotionally disturbed or disabled.

The second reason that we have a soul is also easy to understand.

2. **You have a YOU that is not part of your body.** You can have a heart transplant, but you do not lose your "you." You can have your arm cut off, your legs amputated, but still you do not lose who "you" are. I am something other than any body part like the brain, heart, eyes, limbs, lungs, other organs, and on and on. I say, "This is my arm." The "MY" is separate from the arm. I am not my arm. You can remove my eyes, but they are only my eyes, not ME.

I am something separate, from and something other than my body. It's easy to see, isn't it?

---

9 Remember the story of the Heart Surgeon whose patients could see it all from above even though their body was totally asleep?

Once again, we know intuitively we have a transcendent identity, that we are souls.

3. If this is true, **the SOUL is the true person** that, as St. Augustine states, "rides on the body and uses it but is totally separate from it. The soul has no parts like the body has (arms, legs, heart, brain, etc.) If the real YOU exists in every part of you but has no parts of itself, then it is whole, the real you, the TOTAL you.

All that being said, the soul needs the body and is linked to it forever. In a sense we don't have souls but rather ARE souls -

> *God made humans and they became living souls.*
>
> Genesis 1-2.

God didn't make a body and place a soul in it, but made the unit, completing it by breathing his breath into it and they became living souls.

To sum up then, we see that we are not just material, a lump of flesh but a SOUL - flesh and something BEYOND the flesh that needs to be treated by therapists. We are SOULS - material and immaterial that make up who we are - magnificent creatures made in the image and likeness of God.

When therapists begin to treat the TOTAL person, they will then bring TOTAL Relief. And that's the essence of this book - shining the light on what many therapists fail to see.[10]

---

[10] Much of this is not their fault. They were never trained at the university where they got their degrees to realize the dualism of people - material and immaterial (SOULS). In fact, they were taught against this great truth.

7

SOUL-less Psychology

TOO OFTEN MODERN PSYCHOLOGISTS and therapists treat people on the HORIZONTAL plane rather than the VERTICAL plane. There are too many, even in the Christian field of psychotherapy, who neglect the soul. Both Christian and non-Christian approaches can, without question, be helpful and aid in bringing healing. This book does not discount the skill of trained therapists who work with people who need their assistance and insight.

The thesis of this book is that they do not take people far enough into the depth of their souls so that they can find TOTAL healing.

Imagine helping people on the high and raging seas, giving them aid so their boat doesn't sink, but NOT GETTING THEM TO HOME PORT. The person doesn't drown, but still they are not saved.

What then is the answer to this dilemma?

In the beginning of humanity, God BREATHED into humans his very own breath. Therefore it is easy to conclude that LIFE IS FOUND IN THE BREATH OF GOD.

You recall at the first of this book I wrote about Teresa who's daughter was murdered setting her on a long pathway of depression and internal dismay. Her Christian counselor helped, but did not take her to the springs of living water where she could drink from those life-giving springs that would refresh her soul.

This counselor's education and ultimate PhD in psychology did not equip her to do that. The SOUL was off limits. So she did therapy faithfully in the way she was taught.

Sad, isn't it, that this good Christian woman didn't take Teresa and all of her clients to the source of healing, God himself, to that Holy BREATH - the Holy Spirit who would heal to a depth that would be impossible otherwise?

Because of that, her soul was left empty and alienated from her creator, a God who wanted to heal her soul and fill it with total love, peace and joy…forever!

It was the great St. Augustine who said:

Thou hast made us for thyself and our hearts (souls) are restless until they find their rest in thee.

Jesus said:

Come to me all who are weary and laden with heavy burdens, and I will give you rest for your SOULS.

Matt. 11

SOUL REST.

Now that's where real healing takes place.

Unless this soul is healed and inhabited by God, no ultimate, TOTAL healing will take place.

51

8

———————

How Does The Soul Get Healed?

THE HEALING OF THE SOUL IS SIMPLE in once sense. "Simple," you say? "People are complex. Nothing is simple about helping people find healing."

By "simple" I mean bringing people to God. It's not that we might use a good cognitive approach. I am all for that. Yet we must take people deeper into the SOUL itself if we are going to bring healing.

Let me give you some basic steps to healing the soul.

STEP 1

CONVERSION

IN TODAY'S CULTURE MOST PEOPLE HAVE SOULS THAT HAVE NEVER BEEN AWAKENED TO GOD THEIR MAKER. Our society is basically ignorant of spiritual things and is resistant to any "preaching" about God and conversion.

Religion is no longer in vogue. Instead, it's all about the individual; what can I get out of life with focus on material goods and pleasing the body - eating, drinking and sex, trying to FEEL better with less anxiety and more peace.

This cultural revolution has been in revolt against God for decades now, even a few centuries since the time of the Protestant Reformation where individualism began to rule. Now it's "what's best for ME." The problem is that the "me" does not include the total self which houses the soul. All of that is bypassed in favor of the NOW, getting all one can.

The difficulty is that all of this has brought more and more unhappiness and alienation. With a divided self (the soul pushed aside for the body alone), the drive for fulfillment is too often denied.

So what does modern psychotherapy do? They seek to help bring peace to an internal world that is battling the soul. Can they do it successfully?

Look around. There are millions who purchase CBT books, or see a therapist, but never find true peace within themselves. So they seek thrills, down illicit drugs or smoke another joint. On and on they go never arriving at their ultimate goal.

It reminds me of a song that Peggy Lee sang years ago.

> *Is that all there is, is that all there is?*
> *If that's all there is my friends,*
> *then let's keep dancing*
> *Let's break out the booze and have a ball*
> *If that's all there is.*

So humanity is mostly LOST, and the therapies that seek to bring about a cure are dead end streets. Therapists are LOST themselves because THEY NEVER TREAT THE SOUL within themselves nor the souls of their clients, that internal fabric that links the body and spirit.

So the first step is to acknowledge the insufficiency of modern therapy and to get back to the roots of our humanity, men and women created by a God who loves us and wants the best for each of us.

To do this we must acknowledge:

1. **Our Brokenness.** The word in the Scriptures is one we hate to use today - SIN. We hate to own up to the fact that we have missed God's goal for our lives (a good definition for sin - to miss the mark). Unless we acknowledge this, there is no ultimate hope. We can put bandaids on our brokenness, as is the case with most therapies. This sIn is simply - "I" centeredness that ultimately never satisfies.

2. **The Solution.** Some people know that something is wrong so they run to everything but Christianity. They try Buddhism, or some other religion seeking to soothe their inner being.

That's good - the search for something greater.

Yet, if you read my book, *If There Is A God, Whose God Is God?,* we see that Buddhism is only a start. The ultimate goal, as one climbs the mountain to God, is to place one's trust in Jesus Christ WHO PROVED he was God by all he did and said.

Buddha is dead. Jesus is still alive and promises to come into our SOULS and bring purpose, peace and joy, the kind you can find in no other place.

So the solution is simply this; put one's personal faith in Jesus Christ as Lord and Savior, be baptized so that one can be joined with him in a bond that brings life now and eternal life forever.

If Jesus Christ is the true Savior, then this step is the only viable step one can and should take.

I have encouraged people to spend time reading the Gospel of John, and every time it says, "believe,", do it. This step can bring about an inner revolution in one's life that changes the soul.

If you would like to see another approach to the brokenness of humankind, read another unusual book I wrote called, *THE NOTE - A Visual and Verbal Parable of HOPE & JOY.*

In this book the word, "God" nor "Jesus" is ever mentioned. Yet it shows, in visual ways, God's eternal interest in us, his love and his devotion to us after humanity lost its way, all done through this visual and verbal parable about The NOTE.

If you are a Christian therapist, you cannot force God on anyone, as you well know, but you can guide your clients in this direction as you talk about REAL PSYCHOLOGY (SOULcology) and the soul - how they will never be fixed until they come to the fixer - God himself.

If the only solution to a soul that is alienated from God is to allow Jesus to enter that soul, then bringing that soul into a vital relationship with its maker is of paramount importance.

It is the ONLY WAY to practice true SOULcology.

STEP 2

REDEMPTIVE THERAPY

———

A FTER CONVERSION, WHERE A PERSON ACKNOWLEDGES THEIR BROKENNESS and comes to Christ to find forgiveness and restoration, they need to then truly grasp the significance of the cross. When they do this, they will find healing.

Why?

Why is focusing on the cross so vitally important, a focus that can bring healing to the soul?

There is a great deal of LOVE bound up in the cross. It is here that the foundation of forgiveness and restoration is found.

One of the reasons people get depressed, anxious or fearful and are covered over with hopelessness and despair is rooted in one core belief - God doesn't love them (or no one truly loves them for who they are).

Oh, they think he does in one since, but they cannot conceive how a loving God would let them go through the pain of a divorce, rejection, cancer, death of a dear family member, and on and on.

"If God truly loved me he would have protected me from this horrible experience," they think.

It is this kind of THINKING that I have had to often address in my counseling sessions.   In fact, it was something deeper than thinking.

It was BELIEVING.

Dealing with thoughts is one thing. Dealing with BELIEFS is another.   Beliefs are thoughts that are rooted, foundational to us, and it is from these beliefs that thoughts surface.

So one should not just change their thoughts but their BELIEFS.

The most basic core belief one can embrace to restore their soul and find healing is…

GOD LOVES ME!

I recall when I asked Teresa, the mother whose daughter was murdered and died in such a dramatic, horrific way, "Do you believe God loves you?"

Her reply was almost immediate - "Of course. We all believe that God loves us."

I sat for a moment pondering, thinking what to ask.

Then I inquired: "Teresa, do you believe God personally and totally, without reservation loves…

YOU?"

Teresa sat there for a moment processing what I asked.

"I believe God loves the world, but HOW COULD HE LOVE ME AND LET MY DAUGHTER BE MURDERED IN SUCH A VIOLENT WAY?"

As she spoke tears ran down her cheeks.

This wound that Teresa suffered was raw and deep. Yet I knew she was going to be healed. Why? All I had to do was to help her embrace God's love, no matter what, and make it a strong, towering core belief.

When we talk about love, there are three different kinds. It is important in therapy that a client understands these different kinds of love.

You can relate these kinds of love to yourself or, if a therapist, to a client.

1. **I love you "if" kind of love.** "If you will do this for me, I will love you."

    This is purely conditional love. It puts you under the microscope and examines everything you are and do.

2. **I love you "because of" kind of love.** This is another conditional kind of love, but better than the "if" kind. It goes this way: "I love you because you are beautiful."

    But what happens if in an accident that beauty is marred? Love then evaporates. Or..."I love you because of your sense of humor." Yet, if this person suffers some kind of mental injury either by accident or disease are they still loved?

There is nothing wrong with loving a person because of beauty, humor, or any other positive trait. But this can't be a foundational and an enduring kind of love.

3. **I love you "no matter what" kind of love.** Now this kind of love will last. We want to be loved this way, that no matter what happens, that person who declared their love for us will keep on loving us…"no matter what."

    This is the kind of love that sacrifices for the person loved.

So the question so many ask is not, "Does God really love people but DOES GOD LOVE…

ME?"

That is a question we all ask at times not only for others but for ourselves. If we do not feel someone loves us, our hearts will ache most of our lives, chained to thoughts of inadequacy and fear.

So many die of a broken heart because they do not feel loved. It is one of the basic, essential emotional foods. When we are starved for love, we feel empty, alienated and often worthless.

This is why when we deal with people who are both material and immaterial - SOULS that need to be loved, the therapist is doing their best when they help a client discover and embrace God's love. They need to hear:

God loves **YOU!**

Now let's back up for a minute and be realistic.

Is it true that God's deeply loves each and every person? Or is this only a kind of Santa Claus myth that is just a feel good story that is not in line with reality?

Does God really love people? Does God really love you?

We should not shove this question aside thinking that we are not interested in religion at all. If you do this, you will sweep God from your thoughts which could very well get rid of all meaning and purpose in life.

How can life have any lasting meaning if there is no God, if there is no ultimate difference between us and a rock?

There is none if we are materialists only and do not leave room for that immaterial part of us - the soul.

So we ask those timeless questions: "Why am I here? Who made me? Am I only a composite of organisms that came from an impersonal universe?"

If you believe this, look at my book, *If There Is A God, Whose God is God?* It will help you think through you and God in a very logical way. I think you will like it.

Once you settle the question about God and take a step of a reasoned faith, and believe, you will finally open your heart to a love that can change your life, to the very core - your soul.

Then you will begin to drink in the presence of a God who made you and loves you deeply.

The Holy Scriptures says: *GOD IS LOVE.*

This is essentially who he is…PURE LOVE.

And it's not the kind of love that is an "if" or a "because of" kind of love. Yes, it is true that God gives us laws and principles to live by, but only because he loves us. He never says: "You screw up and I will hate you."

Never!

The Scriptures states this in clear tones.

> *God **PROVED HIS LOVE** FOR US that while we were sinners (doing things that are wrong - things that hurt us and others), Christ DIED for us.*
> Romans 5

Now that's the kind of love to build your life on, the kind to believe in.

God's love is ALWAYS giving.

> *God so loved the world that he **GAVE** his only begotten Son.*
> John 3

"Yet," people say, "if God loved me, why did this horrible thing happen?"

It's like Teresa saying: "If God loved me, why did he let my daughter get murdered?"

You already know the answer, don't you?

There is the age old question that states: "If God loves me and also has all power to stop anything, why did he let this horrible thing (like cancer, death of a child, loss of job, accident that left permanent scars, rape, divorce, etc.) happen to me?

First, God is love. This has been proven on the cross and in so many other ways.

Second, God is all powerful. Creating the universe and keeping it running is a great demonstration of that power. So if God loves you and me, why doesn't he, out of love, and by his power, stop our suffering and pain?

Realize that God often does not stop our suffering and pain because HE DIDN'T STOP HIS SUFFERING and pain. Why? Suffering on his part and ours can be **REDEMPTIVE** and bring about eternal and glorious changes both to us and others.

Let me say that again. You need to get this if you are going to understand your suffering or help your clients with theirs.

God often does not stop our suffering and pain because HE DIDN'T STOP HIS SUFFERING and pain.

Why?

Suffering on our part can be REDEMPTIVE even as it was on his part. By being redemptive it means that it has value in our lives in in the lives of others.

Redemptive suffering is the **Catholic** belief that human suffering, when accepted and offered up in union with the Passion of Jesus, can bring about changes in us or to another covering physical or spiritual needs of oneself or another.

This is why in the Catholic and some other churches, Jesus Christ is still on the cross in full display to all who enter. Why? How grotesque!

Really?

Jesus said:

> *Greater love has no one for another than a person*
> *who gives his life for his friend.*
>
> John 15

This is how much God loves you and me. God GAVE HIS ALL that we might find life to the full.

It is important to understand God's love. If you do not grasp it and bank your life on it, you may ALWAYS struggle with some form of anxiety and depression.

Yes, you can practice reinterpreting every event so that your feelings will change. Great! But that is not enough.

If, you are a therapist and, you want to move your clients into a deeper kind of joy and inner happiness, you need to embrace the LOVE OF GOD and help them do the same. It is the only hope for the soul.

I have sent people to a Catholic Church to spend time before the crucifix. I ask them to spend at least 15 minutes drinking in the love of God.

"Go ahead," I say, "touch his wounds like Thomas did. It was in the touching of the wounds of Christ that he found new life, hope and even a new mission that drove him to India to share the good news about the love of God."

When a person goes into a Catholic Church they will see a red light (a candle) burning. This means that Jesus is present in the Tabernacle - a special place where they put the Eucharist - the actual body and blood of Jesus Christ.

Here's what I tell my clients so that they can drink in and embrace the love of God.

If you kneel before the cross, you can ask this Jesus who is present to show you more fully his love for YOU.

He doesn't just love the world...he loves YOU! Drink it in. And let this be a belief that will be a foundation that will not be shaken.

Say: "GOD LOVES ME!"

Shout it out!

Knowing this will be the beginning of dispelling your depression, anxiety and fear. It is a giant step to healing the soul. All the nasty things that have occurred to you, all the bitter hassles were allowed to touch you so that you might lean more fully on the love of God.

Teresa went to a Catholic Church and was changed in the process. It was there she had a conversion of heart as she realized for the first time the love of God. All the hurt ultimately came to bring her into the arms of a loving God who loved her deeply and wanted her to trust him completely.

Why does God allow hurt? It is ultimately to heal us, to take us to another level in our lives, to reach the mountain top struggling all the way, yet when we make it to the top there is unequalled joy.

Yes!

What love!

Now, think about your life and answer these questions that you need to ask yourself or for a client you may be working with.

1. Have you ever really been truly loved?

2. Who, without question, loves you today, without strings attached, no conditions?

3. Do you really believe that God loves you? If so, why? If not, why not?

4. What is keeping you from embracing his love?

5. Are you willing to go to a Catholic Church and spend time, in front of the crucifix, meditating on Christ's love for you?

6. How can this core belief of God's love dispel your depression anxiety, fear or other emotional issues?

STEP 3

KEEP CONNECTED TO THIS GOD WHO LOVES YOU

LECTIO DIVINA

LECTIO DIVINA IS A SLOW, PRAYERFUL, meditative, contemplative approach to the Scriptures that will help a person connect deeply with God and his love. Today "mindfulness" is often talked about. It is a good thing for anyone to practice. Yet, it can only take you so far to quiet the anxiety and cares of life. This is why Lectio Divina takes people ALL THE WAY, connecting their SOULS to the heart and life of God.

Lectio Divina means "divine reading." It is a very old practice in the Church and goes back to St. Benedict in the 6th century. There are rules you must follow to practice Lectio Divina. It is an approach to Holy Scripture that is:

1. **SLOW.** You are not out to read an entire section, chapter or even a paragraph. You go word by word, drinking in the meaning, pausing as you observe this word of God to you. You don't want to miss anything. You have prayed: "Open my eyes that I may see wondrous things out of your word" (Psalm 119), and you believe that this will come to pass. You are centering on HIM, your creator, your master, your intimate friend.

It may take you a week, two weeks, a month to get through a chapter. But that's OK. It's not how much of the Bible you get through that counts but how much of the Bible gets into you.

This is a treasure hunt where you are looking under every word for that special treasure God has for you. It is like squeezing an orange, desiring to get out all the juice, the sweetness into your SOUL. You are seeking to merge your thoughts with HIS thoughts.

So you quiet your mind, find a place where you can leisurely loiter in the presence of the God who wants to embrace you, guide you, and be your friend.

2. **PRAYERFUL.** It is here in the Scriptures that we meet face to face with God. He wants to enfold us into a deep relationship with him. So we pray, "Come Father, come Holy Spirit, come Lord Jesus and meet me as I drink in your precious words." It is in this process that we find that Jesus will "open our minds to understand the Scriptures," like he did those early two disciples on the road to Emmaus. So as we read the Holy Scriptures, we are always praying, communicating with the God who gave us his Word.

The Scriptures are like a telescope that bring us into the presence of God. Too often people study the telescope, take it apart, know all about how it functions and works. And that may be good, but the ultimate purpose of a telescope is to bring a person into the presence of the stars.

So too the Scriptures. You can study them, memorize them, read them, tear them apart, but until you let them bring you into the presence of Jesus, you are not using them the way they were designed.

This is why, when we open this sacred book, we pray and keep on praying. The words of Scripture are not ordinary words. They are powerful, explosive, life changing. And we cannot come with human understanding and think we will grasp what these words mean. We must tune our ears to the writer of these words, God himself, talking with him, and letting him talk with us.

3. **MEDITATIVE.** At this point we are ruminating, marinating, chewing, rolling over the words of Scripture in our minds and hearts. During this time we are talking with God and letting him talk with us. The "ears on our hearts" like Solomon, are attentive, ready to receive insight, the kind that produces a "burning in our hearts," like it did on those two early disciples with Jesus.

At this point we begin direct dialogue with God, interacting, drinking, eating, breathing in his words, letting our souls consume them, this spiritual nourishment that is vital to our spiritual existence. God is becoming our friend in an intimacy that cannot be described, so deep it is, so close, so loving. We share with him our deepest desires, our hopes, our dreams, our pain, our doubts, our confidence in him. And we listen, drinking in his words in the moment, *rhema,*[11]

---

[11] *Rhema* is a Greek word for "word" but different than "Logos" which refers to the total of God's revelation. Rhema is a more direct communication of God to you. Logos is like eating bread. Rhema is like eating hot bread, just made for you!

hot bread for the soul that results in joy and inner gladness.

King David in Psalm 1, talks about ruminating on the Scriptures day and night. I recommend people memorize sections of Scriptures as they work through them, words of God that they can sift through in their minds and hearts through the day. Like a cow chewing its cud, we can chew on the Word of God, slowly, meditatively, getting out of it all the nourishment that is needed for that moment.

4. **CONTEMPLATIVE.** You are swept into a place of total reverence, praise and joy. You drink it in, not saying anything, not listening at this point, just lingering, resting in HIS presence. There is total silence, yet a communication that goes beyond words taking us into infinity, into the realm of God, into his throne room the holy of holies. It is like two lovers who embrace without saying any words. The moment has swept them into an encounter of their souls. So too with God. He is in us, we in him, in that infinite, finite embrace.

It is like mouth to mouth resuscitation. We receive his life. At this point we may hear the groans of the Holy

Spirit that St. Paul talks about in Romans 8, uttering words that we cannot understand. It is awesome, breathtaking, magnificent, overwhelming and absolutely necessary if we are going to get back to the Garden of Eden where we lost this great gift, communing with and embracing our creator.

This brings about the change we need, a change that breathes into us HIS life - TOTAL UNION with our creator.

To make sure you have sufficient tools so that you can open your SOUL to the breath of God, you can use this helpful approach to opening any Scriptural text found in STEP 4.

STEP 4

USE THE FIVE QUESTIONS METHOD TO READING THE SCRIPTURE

WHEN YOU READ A SPECIFIC SCRIPTURE or focus on the daily readings like The WORD Among Us, MAGNIFICAT, or others, ask the following five questions. They will help you to dig deeper and allow you to benefit greatly with your time with God. It is best to read a paragraph or two as you do this.

Your SOUL will thank you!

1. What is a **KEY WORD,** words or phrase that stands out when I read this passage? Look it up in the dictionary to get its clear meaning or use Biblehub.com. (See appendix on how to use Biblehub.com).

2. In a **SENTENCE** or two, what is the passage talking about?

3. Can I **ILLUSTRATE** what the passage is talking about in my own life or in the life of another?

4. What is Jesus **ASKING ME TO DO** in response to this passage?

5. If Jesus were standing before me right now (and he is!) and asked me: "**WHAT DO YOU WANT** me to do for you?" What would I say?

Write these answers down in your journal. It's life changing!

Jesus stands at the door of your life, your SOUL and wants to come in. Listen to him as he says:

Look. I stand at the door of your soul and would like to come in. I won't force myself in. You must invite me into your life. If you do, I will come in and feed you in a way that you have never been fed before. You will delight in my presence and YOUR SOUL WILL FINALLY BE AT PEACE, HOPE AND JOY!

STEP 5

PRAYER THERAPY
Talking with and listening to Jesus

HOW MANY LIVE THE CHRISTIAN LIFE without Christ? Oh yes, they have the Church - all the activities, going to Church, being involved in the organization, the people, making friends, all the social stuff that goes on. But Jesus? We know who he is, but DO WE KNOW Him?

It is this KNOWING (personal, intimate knowledge) that makes all the difference in our SOULS.

It was John, the disciple of Christ, who wrote in his Gospel:

This is eternal life that they might KNOW...Jesus Christ.

John 17:2

Solomon had just become King of Israel, following his father David, one of the greatest Kings who has ever lived. David, Solomon's father, was called a "friend of God," so close was their relationship. We see that friendship unfold in many of the Psalms King David wrote.

Solomon was a young man who desired to be like his father, to lead his people faithfully.

One night, in a dream, God came to Solomon and said:

Ask anything you want, and I will give it to you.

Imagine. Anything you want!

Most of us would ask for our bank accounts or stock portfolios to be filled with millions of dollars, or to have a new home or other material stuff. Others may ask for a new husband, or for better relationships, for honor, for the recognition we feel we deserve, and on and on.

What would this young king ask for?

84

Notice his request, a deep desire that was life changing.

Give me a hearing heart.
I Kings 3:9

In other words, Solomon asked for a "heart with ears on it." He wanted to be able to hear God's voice deep in the recesses of his SOUL, where God loves to commune with us.

Linda came to me with a depression and void that she couldn't seem to fill. Her husband died of cancer after being married for 37 years. It was over a year now, and the pain of this loss should have begun to heal. But not for Linda. Though she was deeply involved in her Church, it was the times around the home that got to her. The absence of her husband was like a constant dripping faucet. And she sat around the house, moping. [12]

"I don't know what to do," Linda said tearfully. "He was my dearest friend, my soulmate, my life."

---

[12] This story is similar to other stories I tell. There are many situations where I have counseled people who need God in their lives. The names I use in these accounts are fictional only to hide the true identity of those to whom I have ministered.

As I got to know Linda, I recognized a woman who was very committed to her faith. She had been a Christian most of her life and had served God faithfully. Yet there was this hole, this void in her life that gnawed at her soul, a gnawing that wouldn't quit.

Over the decades I have had helping people, I find that as we age, God allows circumstances, events that come into our lives, to prepare us for heaven. He begins to remove those things that have gotten in the way of a deeper relationship with him, the job, raising children, dependance on others, various activities like shopping, sports involvement (tennis, golf, etc.) or other outdoor or social activities. And then there we are…sitting at home with time on our hands.

And that's what God wants…time on our hands.

For he is sitting there with us, wanting a deeper relationship.

Yet too often we ignore him, the source of life and joy. We turn on the TV, read a book, surf the web, or go shopping to deaden the pain of our boredom and loneliness. Day after day that occurs when all the while Jesus is knocking at our

SOUL'S door, asking to come in, to be at home in our lives and for us to be at home with him.

What was happening with Linda happens to so many who not only lose a mate through death, but women who are too busy for a personal relationship with God. They are involved with the Church, but not in a personal, INTIMATE relationship with Jesus.

I turned to Linda and said. "Linda, you are not alone in that house. Someone is there with you who wants to get acquainted with you on a much deeper level."

"What are you talking about," she questioned?

"God."

Linda looked puzzled as she spoke. "But I go to Church, help lead our women's fellowship group, and am on the Church board. What more does God want?"

"YOU," I said softly, trying not to shock her.

"Me," Linda retorted?

What was happening here is what happens with so many women and men. They get tied up with Church, with their religious activities, with the social events of the Church…

Going, going, going…
Doing, doing, doing…

And miss out on the PERSON who wants to get to know them, the founder of the Church, Jesus Christ our Lord.

The Church was never meant to fill the soul. All the activities and great causes, no matter how good, are not meant in the end to satisfy the human heart. Too many get caught up in *"Churchianity"* and miss out on Christianity. They miss out on Christ, like Martha did in the accounts of Mary and Martha in the Scriptures.

Some of you know that I became a Catholic after being a Protestant Evangelical pastor for 35 years and helped grow one of the largest Churches in the Dallas Fort Worth area. Why would I do that? It seemed that I had everything a pastor would want. I did, in one sense. But I knew there was more.

I wanted more of JESUS…in a way I couldn't get him in a Protestant Church.[13]

You see, the central focus of the Catholic Mass is Jesus. The first half of the Mass is focused on Scriptures that lead us to JESUS (one reading from the Old Testament, then we sing one of the Psalms, another reading comes from the Epistles or other New Testament book and then climaxing with a reading from the Gospels where Jesus speaks to us).

After that there is a Homily (a short sermon) on the Scriptures that were read. In all, around 30 percent of the Mass is pure Scripture. St. Paul states to Timothy: "Do not neglect the reading of Scripture."

So the first half of the Mass is Scripture focused, the WORD of the Lord.

The second half of the Mass is focused purely on JESUS, the WORD made incarnate, the Word who came to give his life as a ransom for many. It is here that a miracle happens at every Mass. Bread and wine become the actual body and blood of Christ Jesus our Lord. We see it happen with our

---

[13] For a deeper look, read *The TOTAL JESUS - Why Protestants Get Only Half Of Jesus.* This book is shocking, but based on Biblical and historical truths that are hard to ignore.

physical and spiritual eyes. Jesus comes in a very special way - fully, with his body, blood, soul and divinity.

"The whole substance of the bread is changed into the whole substance of Christ's body, and the whole substance of the wine into the whole substance of Christ's blood. The 'accidents' - color, texture, shape, and so on - remain those of bread and wine. But the substance, the very nature of this reality, is now Christ's body and blood" (St. Thomas Aquinas).

While this happens, we are all on our knees in reverence and adoration. Jesus is here unlike at any other time. It is an awesome occasion, a holy time, as we contemplate His presence. St. Paul says in Corinthians 11, that angels flock to see this event happen because it is so hallowed and divine.

The Mass ends by people lining up to RECEIVE JESUS, actually, physically, totally into their lives - deeply into their SOULS.

The deep magic (words C. S. Lewis loves to use in his books about Narnia) of this event is beyond comprehension. It is what history is all about, Jesus restoring the human race to its place of dignity and divinity.

We all receive the LIFE OF CHRIST as our food that changes us, bringing us back to what we should have been.

Yet, even in this place, in the Catholic Church, millions of people take this spiritual manna and act without understanding. They go through the motions, these sacred actions without being moved in their hearts and souls. And though Jesus is actually present in them, they ignore him, the fountain of life.

It is a tragedy beyond understanding!

No wonder there is so much depression, despair, anxiety and purposeless living. They are blind, men and women living on the animal plane and not rising to and living in that spiritual dimension in the presence of Christ, the one who continues to prove his love for us. To ignore him, to put him on the back shelf is to doom our lives.

So no matter how often you go to Church, you can still miss Jesus. He gets shoved to the side of your life.

No wonder so many have an emptiness in their souls that gnaws at them. Your soul cries for Him, but you stuff it with the busyness of Church, with activities, with shopping, with food, with TV, with so many other substitutes.

In the book of Revelation, chapter 3, Jesus is seen as speaking to a Church, wanting to be part of their lives. All that Churchiness, and too often not much Jesus.

So Jesus says:

Look! I am standing at your souls door and knocking. I will not break down the door and come in. You must open the door and let me in. If you do, we will converse and eat together as friends. We will laugh, cry, and have a conversation that will warm both of our hearts. I am looking for a confidant, someone to talk with. And you need me, for I am the source of life and joy. Open that rusty hinged door. If you do, I promise to come in and fill all your heart's desire.

Revelation 2:20 expanded

How long had Jesus been knocking at Linda's door?

I have found that years and years go by and the tender, determined Jesus keeps knocking. We hear the knocks and, as if there is a solicitor at the door, we ignore him thinking that he will go. After all, we are so busy. There is the book to read, the TV show to watch, the kids activities to go to, a game to attend, and all the Church and social obligations.

But he persists. Knocking. Knocking. Knocking. He wants into your SOUL, to inhabit it and make it his home.

I continued my conversation with Linda.

"I want you to buy a paper back Bible, one you can write in and underline the special things God will be saying to you. You see, if you are going to allow Jesus to be part of your life, if you want him to be your shepherd, you need to daily read and meditate on the Scriptures.

It was St. Jerome who said:

> *Ignorance of Scriptures is ignorance of*
> *Christ.*

So, Linda, you are going to begin a journey into the heart of Jesus and let him speak to you in ways you never thought possible.

I also want you to go to the stationary store and buy a tablet or a diary. This is going to become one of your most prized possessions after a few weeks and months. In this diary you are going to start recording your conversations with God."

Linda sat there, looking confused.

"But I don't have conversations with God," she said. "I pray, you know, the usual prayers for my kids, our Church, my health. But that's about it."

"Linda, I'm going to teach you how to listen to God," I spoke, seeking to encourage her. And then I shared with her the story about King Solomon and his desire to hear God.

"You've got ears. You just need to learn how to use them. Because when you do, you will never have that aching loneliness in your heart again.

Of course you will always miss your husband. But God is using this loneliness you feel to draw you closer to him. He is at the door of your heart and wants to put a balm on your aching soul, and bring joy and purpose back into your life."

Linda turned and spoke with hope in her voice. "I want that more than anything. I want to learn how to use the ears on my heart."

What Linda needed to learn was how to abide in Christ as taught by Jesus in the Gospel of John chapter 15.   She needed to learn how to drink in the sap from the vine, the presence and person of Jesus, dining with him, sharing things in common, being confidants of each other at a depth that would fill the heart with a satisfaction and joy that is uncommon with most Christians, even those who serve faithfully.

Yet this is what we were made for. Adam and Eve had it before sin entered the human race, and since then we have shut God out, leaving him knocking at the door.

All the while there is that ache without him. The soul is thirsty, hungry for God.

> *As the deer longs for streams of water, my SOUL longs for you O God. My being (soul) thirsts for God, the living God.*
>
> Psalm 42:1

An old song in response to that image of Christ knocking at the door of our lives puts it this way:

> *Into my heart*
> *Into my heart*

Come into my heart
Lord Jesus
Come in today
Come in to stay
Come into my heart
Lord Jesus

Linda needed to let Jesus in.

So many today accept Christ as their personal Lord and Savior. They acknowledge their sin, accept Christ's payment for them on the cross and receive that redemptive provision that Jesus made for them. They are then baptized, placed into Christ and Christ into them. But this is just the beginning. Jesus is their savior but hasn't become their personal friend, their confidant, sharing the deepest things together in an openness and honesty that only comes from this kind of friendship.

Linda was going to learn how to go on a treasure hunt into the heart of God - opening her ears to the voice of deity, fellowshipping with God in a way she had never done before. And once she learned how to make that journey into the heart of God, her aching soul would be healed. Linda would never be lonely or suffer from debilitating depression again.

This is the secret to the Christian life, the secret to joy, all found in the Solomon principle - having ears on our hearts, listening to the voice of our Savior, sharing together in this holy friendship and receiving the fruit of it - JOY THAT IS COMPLETE.

That's what Linda wanted, and so do you, don't you? And if you are a therapist, this is what your clients deeply desire.

Well, Linda came back to the next session with her Bible and diary and said:

"Now what do I do to listen to God, to go deeper in my relationship?"

What I told her is in the next chapter.

Buckle your seat belt. This is going to put you into another realm in your spiritual life, a sacred place where you may have never entered before.

STEP 6

BECOMING CHRIST'S CONFIDANT

LINDA CAME INTO MY OFFICE with a new paperback Bible and a nice journal she had picked up at her local book store. She had a smile on her face, telling me that she was ready to get deeper with God. I greeted her, complemented her on the Bible and journal she bought, and then said:

"I'm going to teach you how to listen to God. In fact, the sign of being a true Christian is that we can hear God's voice."

"Linda," I said, "Take your Bible and turn to John 10. I want you to read verse twenty-seven."

Linda fumbled with her Bible, trying to find the Gospel of John. I could tell she was not very familiar with were to look. I helped her find the place and she began to read:

> *My sheep hear my voice. I know them, and they follow me. I give them eternal life, and they shall never perish.*

"Now read verse 2-4," I said.

> *The gatekeeper opens it for him, and **the sheep hear his voice**, as he calls his own sheep by name and leads them out. When he has driven out all his own, he walks ahead of them and the sheep follow him, because **they recognize his voice**.*

"Wow, I've never read this before," Linda exclaimed. "I don't believe that I would recognize Jesus' voice. That frightens me."

"It should," I responded.

"The Christian life is a personal relationship with Jesus, not just a belief system that we practice at Church. After all, 'Faith comes by hearing…' (Romans 10:17) and not just through reading the Scripture."

Then I said something to Linda that would encourage her and take away some of her fear.

"You probably know Jesus better than you give yourself credit for. Within a few weeks you are going to be better at recognizing his voice."

Then I told her a story about an experience I had while working in Sofia, Bulgaria.

I was coming down with friends from Mt. Vitosha when I noticed a disturbing thing. Up ahead were two flocks of sheep, led by shepherds, and they were on a collision course. Within a minute or so the flocks would merge and, I thought, it would be a big mess. We all watched as this apparent catastrophe was about to happen.

Sure enough the flocks merged and became one.

But, to our surprise, something absolutely remarkable occurred. The flocks that merged were all of a sudden two flocks again with each shepherd calling out to his sheep to follow him. They KNEW his voice, and they followed him.

Within a few minutes we were sitting in a cafe having coffee and talking about what we had seen. It brought back John 10, and how Jesus leads us, as it says in John 10:10, to a life that is abundant.

Hearing Jesus' voice is so important.   In John 15, the abiding chapter, Jesus says in verse 7:

If you abide in me and my WORDS abide in you, ask for whatever you desire and it will be done to you.

There are two basic words for *word* in the greek Bible, the original language the New Testament was written in. One is logos. Jesus is called the eternal logos in John 1:1. This refers to all that is revealed - the totally. We are called to believe in this totality, the logos when we become Christians.

But there is another word for *word* that fits in to what I was talking about with Linda. It is the word, *rhema,* a greek word referring to a word that is fresh, spoken at that moment, hot. It's the difference between reading a letter I sent you or listening to me in person. They are both good, but one is fresh, relational, something you can interact with in time and space.

I wanted Linda to experience *rhema,* the words of Jesus spoken to her, to his sheep, personally, fresh words that would guide her life and give her encouragement. I wanted her to take the logos (the written Bible) and allow it to become *rhema* - hot, fresh, the words of God spoken at the moment when she was reading the logos (the written message).

Linda seemed to be drinking in what I was talking about - being a sheep, listening to the voice, the words (rhema) of Jesus.

"How do I do that," Linda inquired? "I want to hear the voice of Jesus, like those sheep heard the voice of the shepherd you talked about."

"Now, Linda, you are going to see that what the prophet Isaiah said is true when he said:"

> *My thoughts are not your thoughts nor my ways your ways.*

"You are going to discover the thoughts of God and his ways or actions."

It is in this step, if we are listening to Jesus, that he is going to give us **His** interpretation of every event that happens to us and **His** action steps to take in response to those events. It is here that His THOUGHTS and His WAYS become our thoughts and ways."

> *His ways were revealed to Moses, his mighty deeds to the people of Israel*
>
> Psalm 103:7

"Moses had a much deeper relationship with God than the average Israelite. They were focused on a God who could do something for them. Their thoughts were selfish thoughts - "give me," thoughts. Moses, however, had become a confidant of God and could interact with him as a friend to a friend. He knew how God worked and even, at times, counseled God!"

"It was King David, a man after the heart of God, a man who knew God's voice in a most intimate way, who wrote in Psalm 25:"

> *Make known to me your ways, LORD*
> *Teach me your paths*
> *Guide me in your truth*
> *Teach me*

"You see, Linda, to know the shepherd we need to know his thoughts and ways. And…WE CAN!"

St. Paul said to the Church at Corinth (I Corinthians 2: 10-12),

> *These things God has revealed to us through the Spirit; for the Spirit searches everything, even the DEPTHS OF GOD. For what human being knows what is truly human except the human spirit that is within? So also no one comprehends what is truly God's except the Spirit of God. Now we have received not the spirit of the world, but the Spirit that is from God, **SO THAT WE MAY UNDERSTAND** the gifts bestowed on us by God.*

"Linda, this is what your heart longs for, these deep things of God. And it is available to you because through your baptism, you received the Holy Spirit who will guide you into all truth."[14]

"I want to show you the process of hearing *rhema*, words of Jesus that he will speak to you in the moment, guiding you,

---

[14] Guided, of course, by the Church's teachings

words that will encourage you, move you, give you insight in what to do."

Linda sat there listening to what I was saying, drinking it all in. Then she spoke:

"I want to do that more than anything."

"First," I said, "set aside a place in your home where you are going to meet God, a place that is conducive for prayer and meditation. Some people will light a candle. Others put on quiet, meditative music, others sit in silence.

If you only did this 15 minutes a day you would spend over 90 hours with God a year!

If you spent time with God this way 5 days a week, you would spend 65 hours with God. This all has a cumulative effect as you get to know God better each day. Spending 15 minutes with someone is not much. But when you spend 65 or over 90 hours with someone, you get to know them very well. And, if you do that for a number of years - you and God will become very good friends, and he will share very intimate things with you."

"But you have to begin," I said, emphasizing the importance of what I wanted Linda to do.

As you read this, I want you to see the great value of spending time with God - abiding in him.   It is THE THING that will help you to become an IMPACT woman or IMPACT man with an abiding JOY that will be unspeakable.[15]

I turned to Linda and said: " We are going to start with a very familiar Bible passage, Psalm 23. Turn to it in your Bible."

Linda found the Psalms and turned to the 23rd chapter.

"Before reading any passage, Linda, it is always good to make sure that the pathway into your heart is clean. If the pipeline is dirty or plugged, you won't be hearing much from God. The intimacy will be broken."

John said in I John 1:

If we walk in the light as Jesus is in the light we will have fellowship with each other and the blood of

---

[15] See How To Be An IMPACT WOMAN, or IMPACT MAN along with the IMPACT WOMAN'S or IMPACT MAN'S Daily Walk

Jesus will cleanse us from all sin...if we confess our sin he is faithful and just to forgive us our sin and to cleanse us from all unrighteousness.

"Linda, a number of Christians never hear from God because of sin in their life. Often this sin is simply the sin of not abiding in Christ, walking with him, fellowshipping on a daily basis, moment by moment. In fact, it is simply the sin of ignoring God - doing our own thing without being conscious of his presence."

"I find a good prayer to prepare me for this is the one King David prayed at the end of Psalm 139:"

Search me oh God and know my heart
Test me and know my thoughts
Point out anything in me that offends you
And lead me into your everlasting ways

"After I examine my conscience waiting for the Holy Spirit to point out my sin and acknowledge that sin to God, I then spend just a moment in thanksgiving for God's grace and goodness. When we come to God with praise on our tongue, he loves that, and he loves to open himself up to us, to confide in us on the deepest level.

As Catholics, the sacrament of confession is a beautiful thing where you will confess your sins to God through a Priest and find total cleansing. The kind of confession I am talking about, however, is daily confession, making sure you are clean before proceeding with an open heart before God.

After examination of my conscience and acknowledging my sin and then thanking God for his grace and forgiveness, I always pray a simple prayer of preparation before I begin to read the Bible.   It's a prayer found in Psalm 119:18:"

Open my eyes LORD, that I may clearly see what
you have in your word.

"St. Paul prayed a similar prayer that you could pray found in Ephesians chapter 1, when he says:"

I pray that the eyes of my heart may be enlightened
to see all that God has for me.
Ephesians 1:18, paraphrased and
personalized

"Linda, God is more interested in this relationship with you than you could ever imagine. You don't have to beg him to show up as you spend time in the Scripture. He will be there, waiting for you to be open to him. In the next few weeks you are going to learn better and better how to listen to him and recognize his voice."

Then I looked at Linda and said: "Now I want to give you an assignment to do before our next session. I want you to spend at least 5 days learning to listen to God using Psalm 23. Here's what I want you to do on each day."

DAY 1: Read in a prayerful way Psalm 23 in its entirety. Write down one word that describes what this psalm is talking about. What is the basic thrust of this psalm? This word will help you focus on that. Be sure and use your journal as you write this down. After you come up with this one word, ask God how this word applies to your life today. Write this down.

When you ask God questions, you can almost be certain that when an answer suddenly comes into your mind, it's God talking with you (you are hearing his voice like the sheep hear the shepherd's voice). Don't question it unless it's not in line with the Christian faith. God wants to speak to you. He is interested in every facet of your life. Let him do it.

After you have heard from God, thank him. Spend time praising and adoring him. This pleases him and will bless you.

DAY 2: Read Psalm 23 again, prayerfully, and underline the key words or phrases that speak to you. Jesus is going to highlight some words or phrases for you and will talk to you about them. Write them in your journal. For example, you might underline every time it says, "my" in the passage, or all the active verbs like, "he leads," "he guides," "he restores," as well as other words or phrases. Look at these key words or phrases and let God speak to you about each one. What is he saying to you about those words. Write it down.

Ask God to be specific. He wants to guide you, to be YOUR shepherd. And he is doing it NOW! Be sure and thank him for what he is showing you.[16]

DAY 3: Today I want you to think through your life and how God has shepherded you. Prayerfully read the psalm and note the ways Jesus made sure that you lacked nothing that you really needed. Write down:

---

[16] The book *The POWER of PRAISE With Guided Journal will help you*.

1. How he made you lie down

2. Restored your soul

3. Guided you

4. Was at your side when you went through the dark valleys

5. How he has provided many good things for you (list them)

6. How he is planning to provide a future joy of spending an eternity with him now and in heaven…forever.

This should be a history of Jesus' movement in your life up to the present.

Think through the segments - childhood, young adult, middle age, retirement. Walk with God through these times, let him show you how he was with you. Write them down. As you do so, praise him for being your shepherd.

DAY 4: Read Psalm 23 again, but this time I want you to go to your Catholic Church. Take your Bible and journal and read it slowly in front of the crucifix. As you enter the Church you will notice a red candle burning up front, by the Tabernacle that houses the actual presence of Jesus in the form of bread that has been consecrated. Jesus is totally there, physically, emotionally, and spiritually.

Jesus wants to talk with you from the cross and from his Tabernacle and will give you new insight to Psalm 23.

Be still. Worship. Listen.

Write down what Jesus is saying to you. Remember that his words will come as impressions to your mind, thoughts that will show up that are not ordinarily there.

Linda, as you see Jesus on the cross, your shepherd, know that Jesus wants you on the cross with him, to give yourself away for others even as he did. He is calling you to be a shepherd to others just like he is to you and all those who follow him.

Who in your family does he want you to shepherd? Who does he want you to love in your neighborhood, your Church? Write this down. Jesus not only wants you to receive his love but to also give it. He does not want you to be just a taker but also a giver - helping to take care of the needs of others.

This is a holy time, Linda. We have talked about ABIDING in Christ. The great fruit of this is LOVE of others.

DAY 5: "Get in your big easy chair. Move it back so you are in a comfortable, relaxed state. As you recline, allow Psalm 23 to become more real to you as you picture yourself resting in the arms of Jesus your shepherd.

Moses said:

> *The eternal God is our refuge and underneath are his everlasting arms supporting you.*[17]
>
> Deuteronomy 33:27

Let God embrace you as your loving shepherd. Breathe in slowly as you remember that the breath God gave Adam and Eve, in the beginning of time, is in you. Let that breath move in and out restfully, deeply, breathing in God's life, breathing out anything that is not of God. This helps you to relax and receive his embrace. Don't say anything. Just be in his loving presence.

At times you can let your mind flow to Psalm 23 and the restoration God wants to bring to your soul. Receive it. Let your soul drink in the presence of the loving, caring God. This time in the chair is a time for contemplation where you don't have to say anything nor does God have to

---

[17] Based on the Hebrew translation. Not all Bibles translate this verse as accurately as it should be.

say a word. You are being together, to be one with each other, to enjoy each others presence.

After a period of 10 or so minutes, write down your impressions and what God may have been doing with you. At the end of these five days you will have begun a journey into the heart of God."

Linda not only agreed to do the assignments, but smiled as I handed her the outline for the 5 days. We prayed and then she left with a new spring in her step. She was going to experience how God wanted her to be his confidant, to live in continual fellowship with the Father, Son and Holy Spirit.

Why don't you do the same assignments. It could make the difference that you are looking for.

As Linda came into my office a week later she was bubbling over with excitement and joy. What a difference a week makes! I smiled as she aggressively shook my hand.

"Tell me how your week went with God."

Linda opened up her journal and began to share.

"The first day I felt a little uneasy. I have never done anything like this before. I struggled with doubts like, 'What if this doesn't work for me?' but overcame them as soon as I dug into Psalm 23.

The key word I wrote down was shepherd. This psalm is talking about all the things the LORD our shepherd does for us.

Dr. Paul, I looked up what a shepherd did in Palestine and it's exactly what the shepherd of this Psalm does. The shepherd is always with his sheep, guarding them, guiding them, making sure they have food and water. As I reflected on Jesus, my shepherd, I asked him if he wanted to say anything to me. All of a sudden, like you said, there were words in my mind that captured my thoughts. I wrote down what Jesus was saying.

> *I love you Linda. I have always been with you as a shepherd, guiding you, guarding you even in the hard times like you have gone through losing your husband. I was there with you when he breathed his last, and you felt so empty. I have always been there waiting for you to come to me and find rest in your soul. You are mine, Linda, and I will never leave you."*

Linda wiped away tears from her eyes as she finished. I could tell that this message from Jesus had deeply moved her.

"Wow. That's great, Linda," I replied. "You were carrying on a conversation with God."

"Yes, Dr. Paul, I was," Linda said with joy written all over her face. "This was a real breakthrough for me."

"What happened on day two," I inquired.

"I did as you said, I underlined key words in the passage, words that spoke to me."

"The first word I underlined was 'nothing', where the psalmist said that with the LORD our shepherd, we lack NOTHING. When I underlined that word I was stopped in my tracks. Nothing meant exactly what it said, nothing. But was that true, I thought? Don't I lack things, particularly a husband that I loved for decades? And my body is beginning to fall apart. I have bad knees, my heart is not working like it should, and I don't sleep the way I used to. Then my three children, they don't seem to care that much about me, are too busy to drop by and chat.

There were other things that came to mind about that word 'nothing'."

"How did you resolve this," I asked?

"I wrote out a question for the LORD. 'What do you mean that if you are my shepherd I will lack nothing?' Then I waited for just a few seconds when a thought came out of nowhere. God spoke, at least I think he spoke, and said:"

You will lack nothing because I am with you. I am everything. When you have me you will have all that you will ever need and more. Your husband is gone, and because he was a faithful Catholic deeply devoted to me, you should not worry about his future as well as your future with him. He has trusted in my grace, and you should too! You have bad knees and heart, and you don't sleep so well. But I am there to give you strength to carry on. And one day I will give you new knees, a new heart, and you will be able to rest like a baby. Your children may not treat you like you desire, but if you follow me fully, if you trust that my presence is always with you, I will take care of your children and make things right. Trust me. I am all you need. Without me you have nothing. But with me you have EVERYTHING, and thus YOU LACK NOTHING!

"Dr. Paul, that was so encouraging, the words of Jesus. My life is radically changing as I learn how to carry on a conversation with God, learning to ABIDE in Jesus. You are right, when I spend time with the PERSON, he gives me the PRODUCT that I desire - JOY!"

"Fantastic, Linda. You have come so far in just a few days of meditation on Psalm 23. What else did you underline on day 2?"

Linda shared with me other words she underlined that meant a lot to her, words like lead, restore, guide, dark valley, my, overflows, dwell, forever. She interacted with Jesus on each of these words and found her living LORD was there to interact with her, dialoguing with her, being her PERSONAL savior, shepherd, and confidant.

When Linda shared with me day 3, it showed that she was continuing to make breakthroughs as she spent time, praying this passage, interacting with Jesus, talking to him, listening, asking questions, waiting for the answers. Linda commented on the six questions I had her cover and how the LORD led her as his shepherd.

1. How *he made you lie down* - Linda focused on the word, "made" and said that God grabbed her attention,

especially after her husband died. This *forced* her to rethink her life as she became depressed and alone.

2. *Restored your soul* - Linda was beginning to find that restoration she longed for as she began to drink from an on-going relationship with God.

3. *Guided you* - Linda thought through her entire life, looking at all the situations that happened to her, her parents, school, work, family, problems - all of it. She had never looked at the way God had guided her, protected her, been with her through all of her life experiences. Linda thought of one time, as a teenager, driving on an icy road. The car began to slip toward a ravine with a raging river below. She knew that this could very well mean death. But then, all of a sudden her car stopped sliding. What happened? She drove home shaking, but happy that she was still alive. On reflecting on that incident, Linda realized that her shepherd was there guiding, protecting, saving her. Then she paused to thank the LORD for his love and constant presence.

4. Was at your side when you *went through the dark valleys* - Linda still felt raw feelings from the death of her husband. At the time she didn't feel Jesus'

presence. But now she knew he was there all the time, to support, comfort, be there to pray to and find strength to make it through that time of grief.

5. How he has *provided* many good things for you (list them) - Linda listed many material things, home, savings, as well as friends and family. As she began to write out her list, Linda said that she even thought of the gift of electricity, or the glasses she wore so she could see better. That opened the door to literally hundreds of things she listed. She drew up a gratitude list - one she wanted to use on a regular basis.

6. How he is planning to provide a *future joy* of spending an eternity with her now and in heaven…forever. Linda smiled as she thought about her shepherd, Jesus Christ, providing for her and her family a future full of hope. As I looked at Linda I could see that her depression was gone as she learned more and more how to listen to and abide in Christ Jesus, her shepherd.

After spending time on this assignment, Linda thanked God for being with her in so many junctures of her life. She asked Jesus to forgive her for not being aware of his

continual presence as her personal, loving shepherd. "I
didn't know you were there," she said.

Then she thought of the picture of the person who asked
God where was he when he was going through all his
struggles. "I see only one set of foot prints," the man said.
Then Jesus answered. "You are right, there is only one set
of foot prints, mine as I carried you!"

As Linda reflected on this, she could sense Jesus saying the
same thing to her, particularly as she faced the death of her
husband and the loneliness that followed. Linda wrote in
her journal what Jesus said:

> *I was with you all the time, caring for you, trying to get
> your attention so that you could trust me more.*

"I didn't know," Linda said, shaking her head.

We both sat there for a moment, thanking God for his
continual presence and not giving up on us.

Then Linda moved on to Day 4, going to her Catholic
Church and praying Psalm 23 before the crucifix.

I had told her that: "Jesus wants to talk with you from the cross and from his Tabernacle and will give you new insight to Psalm 23. Be still. Worship. Listen. Write down what Jesus is saying to you. Remember his words will come as impressions to your mind, thoughts that will show up and are not ordinarily there."

Then Linda thought of the verse in Galatians 2:

I am crucified with Christ, nevertheless I live, and Christ lives in me.

In one sense she was up on that cross with Christ. Jesus' death was her death. And Linda knew that without death there would be no new life.

As Linda knelt there in that sacred space in silence before Jesus, she saw Jesus her shepherd dying for her as well as others. Her shepherd was giving his life so that others could live, a sacrificial giving that brought life to others.

Linda thought of her three children, two boys and a girl who were not really involved at all with their Christian faith. She took them to Church, encouraged them to do what was right, but never was the spiritual leader in the home. "I left that to my husband," she said. "And he was often too busy to get involved."

"As I was looking at Jesus on the cross, I decided I needed to join him and give my life for my children. I wanted them to experience the kind of walk with Jesus I was now discovering. In their religious upbringing I had never helped them to develop a relationship with Jesus Christ. It was Church and not CHRIST - all about doing and not about being."

"I then asked Jesus, 'What do you want me to do to reach my children and bring them back to you?' Then I began to write. Jesus was giving me a plan to bring my children back to the faith."

"What did he say," I inquired.

"Jesus told me to love my children - really love them. I had neglected them for a number of years and, as I said, not been the spiritual leader of our home. So the first thing Jesus wanted me to do was to ask my children to forgive me for being a poor spiritual leader. Then he wanted me to pray specifically for my children each day - pray for their return to the faith.

Last, Jesus told me not to preach at them, but to live out the new life I was learning to live. The more I DEMONSTRATED Christ's love, the more they would be drawn to me and ultimately to the Jesus who is with me."

"Jesus also encouraged me to be a better leader at Church in bringing people there into a personal, daily, moment by moment relationship with Christ."

"That's great," I stated. "It sounds like you are becoming a Psalm 23 person - not only letting Jesus be your shepherd, but learning to be a shepherd to your family like Jesus is to you."

Last, we covered Linda's Day 5 with Psalm 23. You recall she was to get into her easy chair, to recline and rest in the arms of Jesus, letting the message of Psalm 23 sink deep into her heart.

Linda did this, having never done anything like it before. She related what happened.

"I sat in my recliner and made sure my mind was slowing down, and that I was truly resting in the arms of Jesus. All at once Jesus seemed to speak:

Linda said that she closed her eyes and sank deeply into the arms of Jesus. It was so comforting. She felt absolutely secure and at peace.

"It was awesome! I have never felt the presence of God in my life in such a concrete way. For some time I lay there in a state of perfect peace. I didn't say anything and neither did God. But there was no question that we were enjoying each other's presence. It was beautiful and lasted over 20 minutes. I guess this is what contemplation is - to be in the awesome presence of Jesus, drinking in his presence."

Then Linda summed it up.

"What a change in my life this past week as I spent time with Jesus in Psalm 23. I feel like I'm just beginning on a journey into the heart of God. And though I still miss my husband's presence, I'm beginning to realize the presence of Jesus, my LORD, my shepherd. He is always there waiting to have a conversation. My depression is subsiding,

I have renewed hope because I have a friend with me at all times to dispel my loneliness. I'm actually beginning to love my life again as this new joy is beginning to grab hold of my inner soul."

Linda then went on talking.

"Dr. Paul, you have me hooked on journaling. What should I do to keep it up?"

"Linda, I'm so encouraged by what you have discovered this week and the relationship you are developing with Jesus. So here's an assignment to keep you going for next week."

"Linda, read John 15 prayerfully, only a few words at a time or a paragraph at most. Underline any words you think are important. Slow down your eyes - look, observe what the text is saying.

Sometimes I bombard the text with questions: why, what, when, how, where, who? Talk to Jesus about your questions and the words you underline. Sometimes I go to the dictionary or a thesaurus to see other words that are similar that will give me new insight. Peel the text back like you are peeling an onion. There are layers there. Go slow. You don't have to finish John 15 this week. Just begin."

I wrote out what I wanted Linda to do:

1. Read the Scripture (John 15) slowly, prayerfully
2. Underline any words you think are important
3. Use your eyes - look, write down your observations
4. Ask why, what, when, how, where, who?
5. Talk to Jesus about the questions you ask
6. Listen, interact with him, write it down
7. Always ask him what he wants you to do in response to the passage
8. End in praise and thanksgiving

As you read about what I shared with Linda, it would be good for you to to go to John 15 and work through this passage with Jesus by your side. He has things he wants to show you about yourself, about himself, about others.

It will make all the difference!

Step 7

OTHER FORMS OF
PRAYER THERAPY

THERE ARE MANY OTHER DIFFERENT FORMS of prayer therapy that are practiced by trained Christian therapists. Let me list a few without going into detail. This kind of therapy believes that Jesus wants to listen to and heal the disturbed person.

LISTENING PRAYER

1. The therapists asks the counselee to bring a problem to Jesus and wait for his answer. If Jesus is real and alive and lives in our souls, he is there to guide us if we ask him to do that.

   Often a first impression is the voice of our Lord. Listen. Write it down. Discern. Follow. Do this often for guidance. I have encouraged clients to keep a journal where they write down questions to God and wait, in a spirit of prayer and worship, for his answer.

Sometimes it takes a while to recognize the voice of God - like recognizing any voice. But once you have heard it enough, you know.

2. So the client is encouraged to take impressions that come to them as an indication that Jesus is talking to them. In fact, the real counselor is NOT the therapist, but Jesus. He begins to uncover the problem and tells the counselee what to do. With a trained Christian therapist, this kind of approach can be powerful. The person being counseled develops a powerful bond with Jesus as he guides them on a pathway toward recovery.

Let me give you an illustration.

Jennifer was having difficulty with her husband whom she thought was having an affair, but she couldn't prove it.

"What can I do to save my marriage," she sobbed.

"Why don't you ask Jesus," I said?

"How do I do that"?

"Sincerely ask him. Here is a piece of paper. Write out your question to Jesus and wait for an answer. Often it will come as a first impression. Ask. Wait. And write down that impression."

Jennifer paused for a moment, then took my pen and wrote a question down for Jesus to answer. Then she waited, questioning whether this would really help.

Then, boom. She smiled as she began to write.

"Quit nagging your husband and begin to praise him and do things that he would like and enjoy."

Jennifer sat back and confessed that she had spent the last year complaining a lot about her husband's perceived behavior - drinking too much beer, watching too many sports shows, not paying her enough attention, neglecting the kids, and on and on.

"All I have done is berate him. No wonder he doesn't like spending time with me."

"Wow," I said! "You have gleaned some great insight, and it was given to you by Jesus. So what are you going to do?"

"Well I guess I should draw up a list of things I could praise him for and get rid of my list of criticisms. This will be hard because I really don't like him. Yet out of love for Jesus I will do it."

"And then he likes time in the bedroom with me. I have shut him out for months. I can also cook him his favorite dinner, fried chicken with lots of mashed potatoes and gravy. I haven't fixed that dish for him in years because he has gained some weight, and I have not been cooking what he likes."

"So, tomorrow, fried chicken!"

I laughed when she said that. "Frank is going to love this and wonder what happened to you."

"Now, Jennifer, I want you to buy a notebook and begin to ask Jesus questions, listen and write down the answers. There are many other questions I'm sure you have. Write them down and Jesus' answers. We will talk about them more in our next session."

Then I prayed. "God thank you that you care for Jenifer and Frank as well as the children. We praise you that you want them to know your will and will declare it to them, especially to Jennifer as she learns how to listen to you. Amen."

You can see, can't you how this kind of counseling with another person, helping them to learn how to listen to God can be so helpful. And, the counselee does not develop a dependency on you but upon the Lord.

There is no better way!

THE ROSARY

Long before I became Catholic I was with my director over Italy who was Catholic. His wife was a counselor, and he told me that she used the Rosary often to help people overcome anxiety.

After I became Catholic over 20 years ago, I began to realize how valuable the Rosary was, not only as a useful guide in prayer, but for overcoming anxiety and other psychological ills.

The Rosary takes people on a journey through the life of Christ using the Mysteries (5 per day), reminders of our need for Jesus and the prayers of his Holy Mother.

The use of beads, the repetition, and the focus on the Mysteries are great aids in overcoming not only anxiety, but depression (praying the Sorrowful Mysteries) as well as other emotions and difficulties.

I encourage you to buy my book, ***The PERSONALIZED Rosary*** and find out just how important praying the Rosary can be for anyone, especially those who are in the grips of depression and anxiety. The repetition, touching the beads, help to take the mind off of present difficulties and FOCUS, on the Holy Mother and her Son, Jesus Christ. For a period of 20 minutes, people get lost in these prayers - this form of meditation that brings healing to the SOUL.

And that's what it's all about isn't it - HEALING THE SOUL.

The Rosary touches the soul because:

1. We first are praying - and praying impacts our souls. Our SOULS were designed for prayer, breathing in the person and power of God.

2.   We are talking to someone who loves us - our Blessed Holy Mother. Jesus made her the Mother of the Church at the cross when he said to John his disciple - "Behold your Mother." And since was one of the foundational blocks of the first Church, she became a Mother to all who built their lives on this foundation of faith.

3.   We are also talking with Jesus. In fact, when we talk to his mother, she takes all prayers and gives them to her son.

4.   When we pray the Mysteries each day (see The PERSONALIZED Rosary where these Mysteries are explained and where prayers are given to help you pray them in an intimate way) your SOUL is impacted bringing peace, hope and joy to your life.

5.   There is a purification that happens in our hearts and souls as we pray the Rosary when we confess our sins and find forgiveness, restoration and healing. Wow! What an impact on the soul! A clean soul is a happy soul.

6.   Most of all, the Rosary focuses on the one who made us, our creator who wants to **breathe his life into ours**.

Breathe On Me Breath of God

Breathe on me, breath of God:
fill me with life anew,
that I may love as you have loved
and do as you would do.

Breathe on me, breath of God,
until my heart is pure,
until my will is one with yours
to do and to endure.

Breathe on me, breath of God;
Fulfill my heart's desire,
until this earthly part of me
glows with your heavenly fire.

Breathe on me, breath of God;
so shall I never die,
but live with you the perfect life
of your eternity.

Edwin Hatch (1835 - 1889)

STEP 8

The Missing Engine
That Should Drive Our Lives

Let me tell you a story, a parable that will show you why the soul needs to be treated and empowered to do what it does best when connected to its power source - God.

YEARS AGO, THERE WAS A WONDERFUL FAMILY who lived on the outskirts of town. One day the father, Fred, decided he wanted to buy a new car for the family. He had saved sufficient money and went to the dealer and bought a brand new Lexus. It was awesome, fine leather seats, metallic black, the kind of black that shone like the midday sun. The interior, dashboard, everything was the best money could buy.

And he paid in cash!

So after Fred got his car, he pushed it out of the dealership, heading home with a grand smile on his face.

He lived where there were some hills that had to be crossed, and Fred, because the car was heavier than the last car, had trouble pushing his new Lexus up the hill. But, with determination, he made it. And did he ever enjoy going down the hills. He would get inside and coast until the car stopped.

It was awesome - this new Lexus!

And his family loved the car - the shiny exterior, the smooth leather seats, the way it handled the bumps in the road. And the radio and stereo systems, they were awesome. As Fred pushed the car through the countryside, they would listen to their favorite music with smiles on their faces.

But all wasn't well for Fred. This car was heavier than the last. He was getting worn out pushing this beautiful car to town, to church, to his work. In fact, Fred was getting exhausted.

Then one day, Fred heard of a seminar on how to push your car. So he went and learned the latest techniques - how to put your back into it, the proper use of your arms and legs, and other secrets to helping you get from point A to point B without getting so tired.

So Fred went home encouraged. He loved his new Lexus, but soon found out, that even with his new techniques, he was still getting worn out. He even had thoughts of parking his new Lexus and walking.

Then one day, he took the family to church as he did every Sunday. And there they came, everyone pushing their cars into the parking lot - tired, sweaty, worn out.

The church had a guest speaker that day who talked about the weariness of those in attendance. Then, to finalize his message, he took the congregation out to their cars. He asked Fred to open the hood of his new, black Lexus. Fred did so with pride.

"Isn't that nice and shiny," Fred said with a smile.

"Yes it is," the speaker replied.

Then this guest speaker asked Fred for his keys. Oh, Fred loved his keys. He could lock his car and open it up just by pushing some buttons. They were magical.

The speaker took the keys and put them into the ignition and turned them. All of a sudden there was a noise that Fred had never heard before. He straightened up, startled.

"What's that sound?" Fred asked, looking puzzled.

"That's an engine," the speaker said, as all the congregation looked on.

"This engine is there to power your Lexus. You don't need to push it any more. You don't need to put your back to it and get worn out any longer. This car was designed for you to sit, relax, and let the engine do the work. All you need to do is turn it on!"

Fred crawled into his new Lexus as the engine was purring. He shut the door and put his foot on the gas pedal. All of a sudden he felt the power moving him forward. It was awesome!

As he sped around the parking lot, the congregation cheered, and they all ran to their cars and opened the hoods, staring at an engine that was designed to run that car without any effort on their part. They just had to turn the key!

The key?

Helping people understand they have a soul that will power their lives when connected to God, the breath, the fuel that makes the soul alive, awake and fully animated.

STEP 9

The Miracle Of Praise

WHEN YOU DISCOVER TRUE PSYCHOLOGY AND THE VALUE OF YOUR SOUL, you will never be the same. You will begin to develop a relationship with your creator, the one who started the human race by BREATHING INTO THEM, and they became living souls.

Once you understand the magic of this, this depth that is missed in most therapy sessions in the world, you will begin to come to a place where true healing will occur. Your soul will be finally liberated to become all the creator intended - and that will free it to find, as the Psalmist said:

PLEASURES FOR EVER!

Psalm 16

When you begin to feel this joy, your heart will begin to sing praises to God. He, your eternal lover, has satisfied your soul and you lift up your hands, clap, shout, blast the trumpet as you praise him.

Look at all the praise Psalms in Scripture. They come from hearts that are full and overflowing with gratitude to God.

There is something magical that happens to you when you begin to praise God. A power is released in your mind and emotions that cannot be matched by any other exercise.

People take drugs to imitate this kind of feeling. And they may get it for a moment or two. Then, back to the drugs for another hit - hoping, grasping, longing for a joy that will never end.

But in God is FULLNESS of joy. Living in HIS PRESENCE, breathing in his nature is all that is needed to release the human spirit to fly high, to move beyond the grips of depression and despair.

Praise.

There is such power in it.[18]

Praise the LORD (Psalm 150)

Hallelujah!
Praise God **in** His sanctuary
Praise Him **in** the firmament of his power
Praise God **for** His mighty acts
Praise Him **according to** His abundant greatness
Praise Him **with** the blast of the horn
Praise Him **with** the psaltery and harp
Praise Him **with** the timbrel and dance
Praise Him **with** stringed instruments and the pipe
Praise him **with** the loud-sounding cymbals
Praise Him **with** the clanging cymbals
Let every thing that hath breath
PRAISE THE LORD!
Hallelujah!

You may also want to praise God in music. Sing to him.
Put on some CD's or any other way to get music into the

---

[18] See book *The POWER Of PRAISE* With Guided Journal. It's one of
those "Life Changing" books.

room, into your soul. As you play, you can dance, clap your hands, grab two pot lids and clang them together.

Go wild.

Let yourself loose and praise the LORD!

<h1 style="text-align:center">9</h1>

Final words

WE BEGAN THIS BOOK TALKING about how modern psychology has lost its way by neglecting the soul. I have sought to demonstrate that all humans have a SOUL, a soul that needs to be inhabited by God.

We have taken you on a journey with illustrations as to how to repair the soul so that it is in tune with the creator, God the Father, Jesus Christ his Son and the Holy Spirit.

If therapists did this, they would help to transform the human race - or better yet, let God transform all of humankind.

So you are a Christian therapist. Will you commit to doing all you can to treat the WHOLE person before you - that SOUL that needs union with God its maker?

And if you are in treatment, don't run from someone who is helping you. Yet, remember, that a clinical psychologist is too often trained to treat part of you - not the TOTAL you. Find, if you can, someone who will take you ALL THE WAY so that your soul will be healed.

For the glory of God.

Amen.

FREE BOOKS
For
YOU!

Be sure and go to <u>DrPaulYoung.com</u> and sign up for a **free book**, a book designed to take you to a new level in your walk with God.

And keep watching this site because new free books will be offered periodically.

Last, **pray for our ministry**. We are seeking to change the hearts and souls of thousands of people around the world and need your prayers.   Send me a note at <u>pauljyoung@mac.com</u> if you will pray for us.

Thanks, and God bless you!

Dr. Paul J. Young

Education:

University of California, Fresno, B.A in English

Dallas Theological Seminary, Th.M (Masters in Theology)

Biola University, Doctorate of Ministry with emphasis on psychology (working with Talbot School of Theology, Rosemead School of Psychology and other schools). Dr. Young's Doctoral degree is not in Clinical Psychology but rather in Pastoral Psychology.

Dr. Paul Joseph Young

Dr. Young helped grow one of the largest churches in the Dallas/Ft. Worth area as its pastor, working with thousands of people, developing his skills both as a minister, theologian, communicator and a counselor (pastoral psychology), working with hundreds of people and developing his unique therapy techniques.

For seven years he was C.E.O. of Community Bible Study International, working in over 60 countries of the world, sharing his message of truth, hope and joy. He held seminars on anxiety, anxiety, stress, fear, anger, and a host of other topics, seeking to bring healing to the thousands in need.

Dr. Paul's communication skills has made him a favorite speaker around the world. He lives with his wife and best friend, Diane. They have five children and 14 grandchildren.

More than anything, Dr. Paul lives to help people find the joyful, peaceful life they deserve.

This is a

<u>DrPaulYoung.com</u>

Publication

———————————

Changing people…

one SOUL at a time!

———————————

www.ingramcontent.com/pod-product-compliance
Lightning Source LLC
Chambersburg PA
CBHW051306250726
48656CB00004B/1511